THE OFFICIAL
TOTTENHAM HOTSPUR
ANNUAL 2026

The 2024/25 season culminated in victory over Manchester United in the UEFA Europa League Final and memorable scenes in N17 a few days later as our players paraded the trophy we won in Bilbao!

The Official Tottenham Hotspur Annual 2026 takes an in depth look back at the 15 Europa League matches in 2024/25 en route to us collecting our first European silverware since 1984. We also review our league and domestic cup performances during the campaign, which included a run to the semi-finals of the Carabao Cup, while we find out how Spurs Women got on in their three domestic competitions.

Elsewhere, this Annual profiles the players who make up our Men's and Women's first team squads while we have an exclusive interview with Spurs fan and music star Kidwild. There are puzzles to solve and a Super Spurs Quiz to test your knowledge of your favourite club and plenty more besides.

Enjoy your new Annual and COME ON YOU SPURS!

#COYS

Andy Greeves

06	Winners - 2024/25 UEFA Europa League Review
14	2024/25 Premier League Review
19	2024/25 Carabao Cup and FA Cup Review
22	2024/25 Barclays WSL Review
28	Crossword
29	Wordsearch
30	Thomas Frank Profile
32	Men's Player Profiles
40	Martin Ho Profile
42	Women's Player Profiles
48	2024/25 Player of the Season Awards
50	Pre-season Training – Summer 2025
52	Pre-Season Round-up – Summer 2025
54	Kidwild Interview
58	Super Spurs Quiz
60	Quiz/Puzzle Answers

2024/25 UEFA EUROPA LEAGUE
WINNERS!

Editor Andy Greeves looks back on our triumphant 2024/25 UEFA Europa League campaign, which culminated in victory over Manchester United in the final in Bilbao on 21 May, 2025

Spurs 3-0 Qarabağ

League Phase – Matchday 1 – 26 September, 2024

We got off to a winning start in the new-look UEFA Europa League (UEL), which featured a 36-team league and eight fixtures per club. We shrugged off the disappointment of losing Radu Drăgușin to a straight red card in the eighth minute as Brennan Johnson netted in the first half – scoring for the third straight game – before Pape Matar Sarr and Dominic Solanke struck after the interval.

Spurs: Vicario, Gray, Drăgușin, van de Ven, Davies, Bissouma (Bentancur 71), Sarr, Bergvall (Udogie 12), Johnson (Kulusevski 46), Solanke (Moore 85), Son (c) (Werner 71)

Ferencváros 1-2 Spurs

League Phase – Matchday 2 – 3 October, 2024

Johnson's red-hot streak continued as he got his fifth goal in five games in our 2-1 victory in Hungary. Like Johnson, who netted on 86 minutes at the Groupama Arena, Sarr made it two goals in two in the UEL when he opened the scoring from close range after 23 minutes. There was a slightly nervy finish when Barnabas Varga slid home a cross from Cristian Ramirez as the clock ticked into five minutes of added time but we held on for the win.

Spurs: Vicario, Pedro Porro, Gray, Romero (c), Davies, Bergvall (Maddison 65), Bissouma, Sarr (Solanke 82), Werner (Johnson 65), Lankshear (Kulusevski 65), Moore

LEAGUE PHASE

Spurs 1-0 AZ

League Phase – Matchday 3 – 24 October, 2024

Our third consecutive UEL league phase victory came courtesy of a Richarlison penalty. Marking his first start since May 2024, the Brazilian calmly clipped a spot-kick down the middle of the goal in front of the South Stand after 53 minutes at Tottenham Hotspur Stadium after Lucas Bergvall was upended by Maxim Dekker.

Spurs: Vicario, Pedro Porro, Romero, van de Ven (Gray 61), Spence, Sarr, Bergvall (Davies 85), Maddison (Bissouma 77), Odobert (Johnson 78), Solanke, Son (c)

Galatasaray 3-2 Spurs

League Phase – Matchday 4 – 7 November, 2024

Our only UEL league phase defeat in 2024/25 came at the intimidating Rams Park in Istanbul. Teenage striker Will Lankshear scored his first goal in our colours to cancel out a stunning opening goal from Yunus Akgun, only for the 19-year-old's night to end in disappointment after he was sent off for two bookable offences in the second half.

Victor Osimhen struck twice in eight minutes before Dominic Solanke came off the bench to reduce the deficit.

Spurs: Forster, Pedro Porro, Drăgușin, Davies, Gray, Bergvall (Solanke 66), Bissouma, Maddison (Sarr 66), Johnson (Bentancur 46), Lankshear, Son (c) (Kulusevski 46)

LEAGUE PHASE

Spurs 2-2 Roma

League Phase – Matchday 5 – 28 November, 2024

We got off to the perfect start against Italian giants Roma when Heung-Min Son converted a fifth-minute penalty at Tottenham Hotspur Stadium. We were pegged back when Evan N'Dicka headed home but regained the lead prior to the break courtesy of Brennan Johnson's third goal in that season's competition. Both sides hit the woodwork in the second period before Mats Hummels earned Roma a point in stoppage time with a close-range finish.

Spurs: Forster, Pedro Porro, Drăgușin, Davies, Gray, Sarr (Bissouma 69), Bentancur (Bergvall 77), Kulusevski, Johnson (Maddison 69), Solanke, Son (c) (Werner 78)

Rangers 1-1 Spurs

League Phase – Matchday 6
– 12 December, 2024

After a goalless first half, Rangers took the lead in the all-British clash at Ibrox shortly after the interval through Hamza Igamane. We levelled on 75 minutes thanks to an excellent team goal that was finished by substitute Dejan Kulusevski, giving us a vital and well-earned point.

Spurs: Forster, Pedro Porro, Drăgușin, Gray, Udogie, Bentancur (Sarr 61), Bissouma (Bergvall 61), Maddison, Johnson (Solanke 60), Son (c), Werner (Kulusevski 46)

Spurs 3-0 IF Elfsborg

League Phase – Matchday 8
– 30 January, 2025

Young forwards Dane Scarlett, Damola Ajayi and Mikey Moore all scored their first Spurs goals as we defeated Elfsborg 3-0 to secure a place in the last 16 of the UEL. Substitute Scarlett put us ahead on 65 minutes with a smart header. And just three minutes into his senior debut, fellow sub Ajayi made it two before Moore rounded off the victory with a stoppage time strike.

Spurs: Austin, Pedro Porro, Gray, van de Ven (Drăgușin 46 (Scarlett 65)), Davies, Sarr, Bentancur (Bissouma 46), Bergvall, Moore, Richarlison (Ajayi 81), Son (c) (Kulusevski 46)

Hoffenheim 2-3 Spurs

League Phase – Matchday 7
– 23 January, 2025

Goals in both halves from Heung-Min Son helped us take a huge step towards automatic qualification for the last 16 of the UEL as we won 3-2 at the Rhein-Neckar Arena. James Maddison put us in front just three minutes into the match while Anton Stach and David Mokwa got goals back for the hosts after each of Sonny's efforts.

Spurs: Austin, Pedro Porro, Drăgușin, Davies, Gray, Bergvall, Bentancur, Maddison (Olusesi 89), Kulusevski, Richarlison (Moore 56), Son (c) (Lankshear 79)

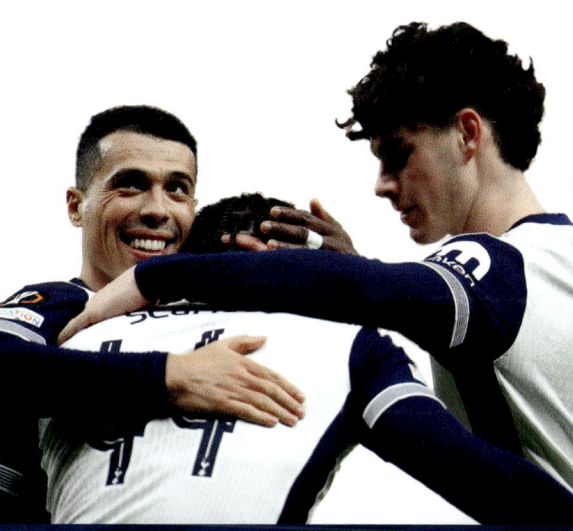

ROUND OF 16

AZ 1-0 Spurs

Round of 16 – First Leg – 6 March, 2025

A disappointing performance at the AFAS Stadion saw us slip to a first leg defeat as we met Dutch side AZ again in the knockout stages. The good news was we departed the Netherlands just a goal down - after Lucas Bergvall inadvertently sliced Troy Parrott's effort into his own net on 18 minutes – meaning the tie was very much alive still ahead of the second leg in N17.

Spurs: Vicario, Spence, Gray, Danso, Udogie (Pedro Porro 72), Bergvall, Bentancur, Maddison (Sarr 72), Johnson, Tel (Odobert 46), Son (c) (Solanke 72 (Scarlett 90+2))

QUARTER-FINAL

Spurs 1-1 Eintracht Frankfurt

Quarter-final – First Leg – 10 April, 2025

Hitting the woodwork twice and forcing a string of wonderful saves from Brazilian goalkeeper Kaua Santos, our performance against Eintracht Frankfurt probably merited more than a draw. Both goals arrived in the first half as Pedro Porro's clever flick cancelled out Hugo Ekitike's early opener for the German side, who finished third in the Bundesliga in 2024/25.

Spurs: Vicario, Pedro Porro, Romero, van de Ven, Udogie (Spence 79), Bergvall, Bentancur, Maddison (Sarr 79), Johnson, Solanke (Richarlison 88), Son (c) (Tel 79)

SEMI-FINAL

Spurs 3 -1 Bodø/Glimt

Semi-final – First Leg – 1 May, 2025

We made a blistering start against UEL surprise package Bodø/Glimt when Brennan Johnson headed us in front inside the first minute. James Maddison added a second before the break and we were totally in command when Dominic Solanke converted a second-half penalty to send Tottenham Hotspur Stadium wild before the mood was dampened slightly when our advantage was reduced seven minutes from time by Ulrik Saltnes.

Spurs: Vicario, Pedro Porro, Romero (c), van de Ven, Udogie, Bissouma, Bentancur, Maddison (Kulusevski 65), Johnson, Solanke (Odobert 75), Richarlison (Tel 46)

Spurs 3-1 AZ
(Spurs win 3-2 on aggregate)

Round of 16 – Second Leg – 13 March, 2025

Wilson Odobert's first goals for the club – on 26 and 74 minutes respectively – and James Maddison's precision strike just after the break saw us turn around our first leg deficit and progress to the quarter-finals. Peer Koopmeiners made it 2-2 on aggregate just after the hour mark before Odobert's all-important second strike of the evening.

Spurs: Vicario, Pedro Porro, Romero, van de Ven (Gray 61), Spence, Sarr, Bergvall (Davies 85), Maddison (Bissouma 77), Odobert (Johnson 78), Solanke, Son (c)

Eintracht Frankfurt 0-1 Spurs
(Spurs win 2-1 on aggregate)

Quarter-final – Second Leg – 17 April, 2025

Ange Postecoglou said he was 'super proud' of our players after they delivered one of our great European performances to beat Eintracht Frankfurt. Dominic Solanke's first-half penalty was enough to make it a glory, glory night in Germany as we produced a superb defensive display in the second period to keep out everything the hosts could throw at us at Deutsche Bank Park.

Spurs: Vicario, Pedro Porro, Romero (c), van de Ven, Udogie, Bergvall, Bentancur, Maddison (Kulusevski 45+1), Johnson (Danso 85), Solanke, Tel (Sarr 79)

Bodø/Glimt 0-2 Spurs
(Spurs win 5-1 on aggregate)

Semi-final – Second Leg – 8 May, 2025

Pre-match, there were concerns that an artificial surface and chilly conditions in deepest northern Norway would be tough to negotiate at Bodø's Aspmyra Stadium. But we did everything right on the night – defended well, showed great character and commitment, and scored two second half goals, from Dominic Solanke and Pedro Porro - to book our place in the UEL Final against Manchester United at Bilbao's San Mamés Stadium.

Spurs: Vicario, Pedro Porro, Romero (c), van de Ven, Udogie, Bentancur, Bissouma, Kulusevski, Johnson (Sarr 68), Solanke, Richarlison (Tel 61)

Spurs 1-0 Manchester United

Final - San Mamés Stadium, Bilbao – 21 May, 2025

It was 'Johnson again' as we achieved European glory on a never-to-be-forgotten night in Bilbao in May 2025.

Our Wales international forward wrote his name into Club folklore with the winning goal three minutes before half-time as we claimed our first European title in 41 years and our first major trophy since 2008. As we had to do in other matches during our triumphant UEL run, there were times when we had to defend resolutely in the final to see out the win. Micky van de Ven's incredible goal-line clearance from Rasmus Højlund was one of the iconic moments of the night while the Dutchman's centre-back comrade Cristian Romero - captain from the start with Heung-Min Son on the bench - was named Player of the Match by UEFA.

Referee Felix Zwayer's full-time whistle was greeted by incredible scenes of celebration – and tears of joy – as we ended the 2024/25 season by winning a major European competition. Glory Glory Tottenham Hotspur!

FINAL

Spurs: Vicario, Pedro Porro, Romero (c), van de Ven, Udogie (Spence 90), Bentancur, Bissouma, Sarr (Gray 90), Johnson (Danso 78), Solanke, Richarlison (Son 66)

Manchester United: Onana, Yoro, Maguire, Shaw, Mazraoui (Dalot 84), Casemiro, Bruno Fernandes (c), Dorgu (Mainoo 90+2), Amad Diallo, Højlund (Zirkzee 71), Mount (Garnacho 71)

AIA
AIA

WINNERS

BILBAO FINAL 2025

AIA
BILBAO FINAL 2025

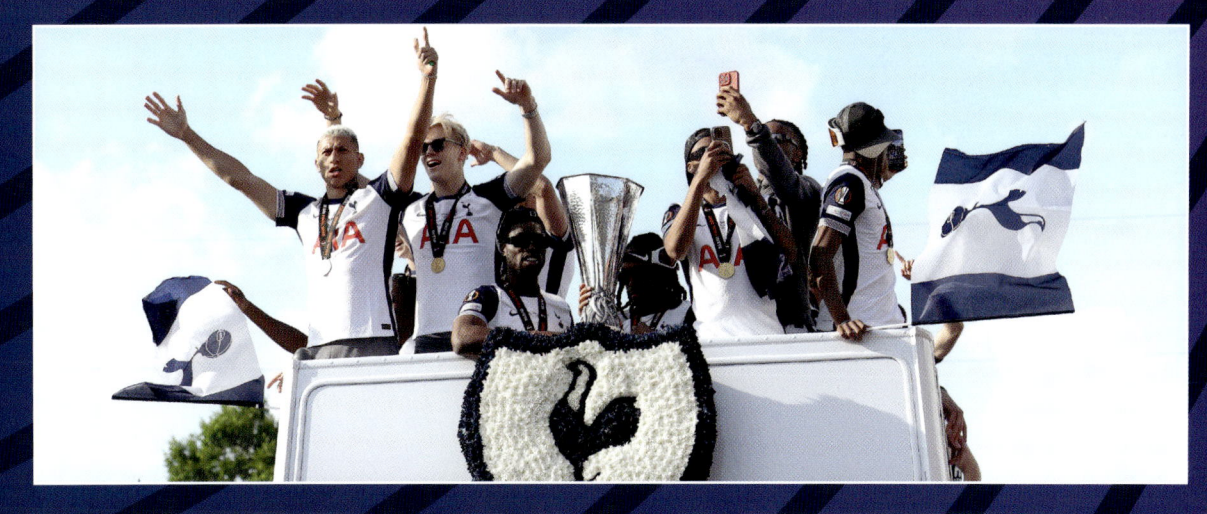

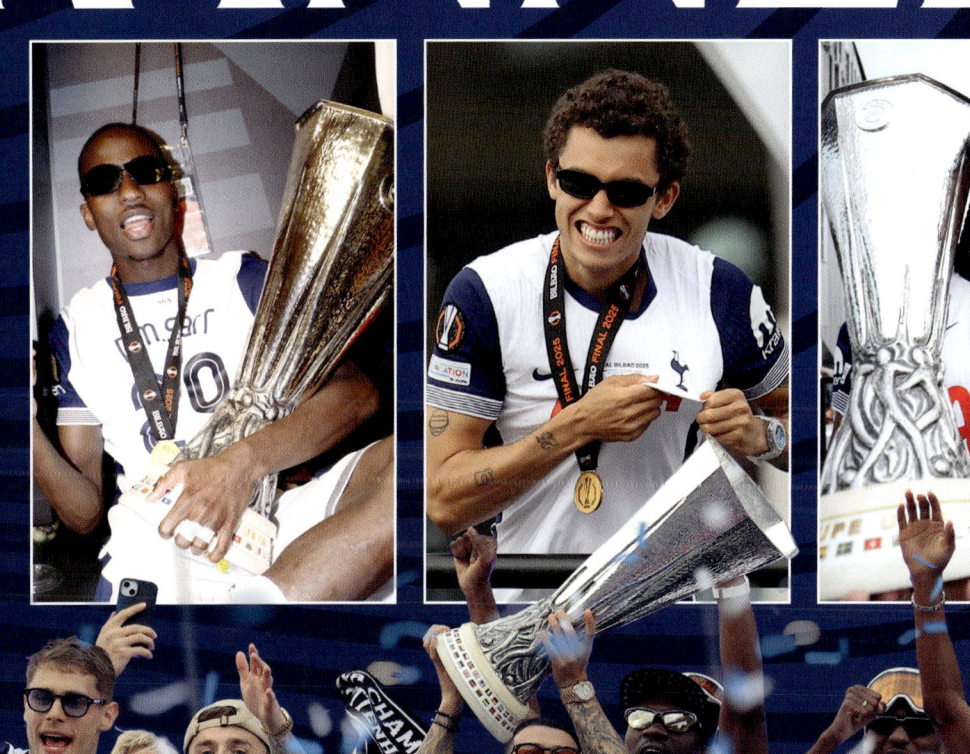

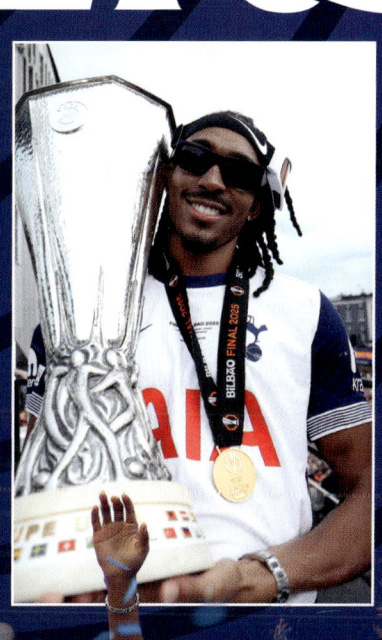

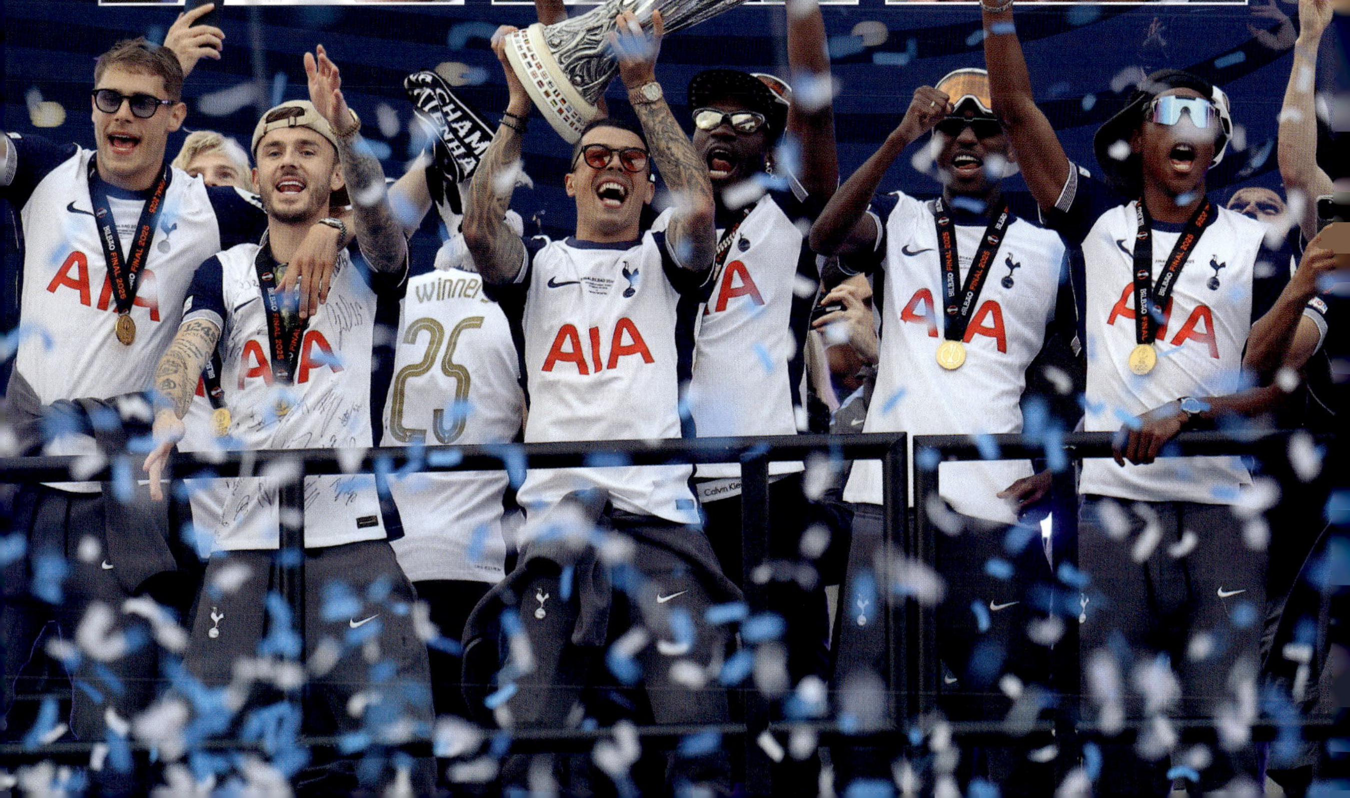
AIA
AIA
winners
25
AIA
AIA
AIA
AIA

PREMIER LEAGUE

SEASON REVIEW

2024/25

While 2024/25 was a glorious season for the Club in Europe, our league campaign was disappointing as we recorded our lowest finish and points tally of the Premier League era.

The season wasn't without its highlights though. We achieved home and away victories over Manchester United, won 4-0 at then-reigning champions Manchester City and we scored four goals or more in triumphs over Everton, West Ham United, Aston Villa, Ipswich Town and Southampton.

August

We made a solid start to the Premier League season, taking four points from a possible six in August. Pedro Porro's goal gave us a first half lead at Leicester City, where we had further chances to put the game beyond the newly promoted team. But Jamie Vardy equalised in the second half to secure a point for the Foxes.

A crowd of 61,357 were present at Tottenham Hotspur Stadium for our first home match of the season, which saw us thrash Everton 4-0. Yves Bissouma gave us the lead on 14 minutes with a fierce drive and Heung-Min Son made it two nine minutes later as he capitalised on a goalkeeper blunder from Jordan Pickford. Cristian Romero's header and Sonny's second goal of the afternoon in the second half wrapped up the win.

September

A 1-2 defeat at Newcastle United, where we benefitted from a Dan Burn own-goal, was followed by a 0-1 home loss to Arsenal in the north London derby. But we bounced back from those disappointments with back-to-back victories. We recovered from going 0-1 down to an early Bryan Mbeumo goal to beat Brentford 3-1 in N17. Goals from Dominic Solanke and Brennan Johnson had us 2-1 up by the break and James Maddison's finish after a great team move on 85 minutes made sure of the three points.

A dominant display from start to finish saw us win 3-0 at Manchester United at the end of September. As was the case so often during the 2024/25 season, Johnson was in the right place at the right time to tap in at the back post at Old Trafford after a marauding run and cross from Micky van de Ven. A few minutes after the break, Johnson turned provider as Dejan Kulusevski prodded his square pass home. Solanke got on the end of Pape Matar Sarr's flick-on from a Lucas Bergvall corner to make it three on 77 minutes.

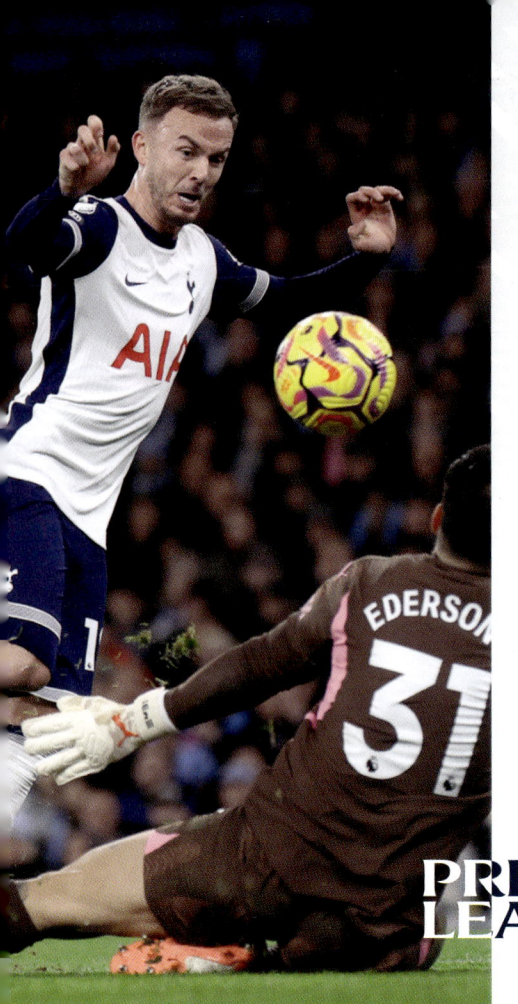

October

Despite goals from Johnson and Maddison putting us 2-0 up at half-time at the American Express Stadium, we ended up losing 2-3 to Brighton & Hove Albion in early October. But the lads once again followed a disappointment with a resounding victory. All five goals in our 4-1 home victory over West Ham United were scored in the opening hour. After Mohammed Kudus gave the visitors an 18th-minute lead, Kulusevski's shot from the edge of the Hammers' penalty area ensured we went in level at the break. Strikes from Bissouma and Son and an own-goal from Alphonse Areola made it a comfortable afternoon for us in the end.

The month ended with a 0-1 defeat at Crystal Palace.

PREMIER LEAGUE

November

For the second time that season, we followed a league defeat with a 4-1 triumph over a team in claret and blue at Tottenham Hotspur Stadium! This time it was Aston Villa who were on the wrong end of Ange Postecoglou's free-scoring Spurs. Son's exceptional cross for Johnson to score – and cancel out Morgan Rogers' opener for Villa – set us on the way early in the second half. A quick-fire brace from Dominic Solanke put the game beyond the Midlanders and James Maddison topped a memorable afternoon with a fourth goal in stoppage time from a free-kick.

Our yo-yo form continued throughout November. A 1-2 home defeat to Ipswich Town – which saw Rodrigo Bentancur score his first goal of the season – was quickly forgotten as we won 4-0 at Manchester City the following weekend. Maddison scored twice in the opening 20 minutes at the Etihad Stadium. Two swift, second half breaks saw us increase our lead as Porro and Johnson respectively were there to provide the finishes.

That win at City increased our goal tally to 27 goals from our opening 12 league games - our best return at that stage of a Premier League season (2.25 goals per game) since the formation of the division in 1992/93. We were top of the scoring charts at that point - three ahead of league leaders and eventual champions, Liverpool, who had 24.

December

It was 'Johnson again', as the Welshman scored his 10th of the season in all competitions to put us one up against Fulham in N17. But Tom Cairney's strike on 67 minutes gave the west Londoners a share of the points.

A 0-1 defeat at AFC Bournemouth was followed by a crazy game at Tottenham Hotspur Stadium that eventually saw us beaten 3-4 by Chelsea. Our goals on the day were scored by Solanke, Kulusevski and Son.

Our biggest win of the season came at Southampton in mid-December as we scored all five of our goals in a 5-0 victory in the first half. Indeed, strikes from Maddison, Son, Kulusevski and Sarr had us 4-0 up after 25 minutes while Madders got his second and our fifth in first half stoppage time.

The goals kept coming but sadly, we were on the wrong end of a 3-6 defeat to Liverpool in N17 three days before Christmas. Maddison, Kulusevski and Solanke all increased their scoring tallies against the Reds. A 0-1 Boxing Day defeat at Nottingham Forest was followed by a 2-2 draw at home to Wolverhampton Wanderers as Bentancur and Johnson netted in the first half. But a missed penalty from Son and a late Jørgen Strand Larsen equaliser meant we missed out on three points.

January

January was a month to forget as we suffered four consecutive defeats. We lost at home to Newcastle United (1-2) and Leicester City (1-2) and were beaten on the road at Arsenal (1-2) and Everton (2-3). Solanke (v Newcastle), Son (v Arsenal) and Kulusevski (with a beautiful, chipped finish against Everton) scored during the month while Richarlison was on target against his former club, Everton, and Leicester.

February

Three wins out of four in February saw us get our Premier League campaign back on track. An own-goal from Vitaly Janelt and a late Sarr strike gave us a 2-0 victory at Brentford. The third of our four wins over Manchester United in all competitions during the season came courtesy of a Maddison goal in N17. And a Johnson brace, plus efforts from Djed Spence and Kulusevski saw us triumph 4-1 at Ipswich Town before the month ended with a 0-1 home defeat to Manchester City.

March

We came from 0-2 down to draw 2-2 with AFC Bournemouth at Tottenham Hotspur Stadium. A long-range effort from Sarr and a cheeky 'Panenka' penalty from Son gave us a point. The following weekend, we were beaten 0-2 at Fulham.

April

We suffered another defeat in west London at the start of April, going down to a 0-1 loss at Chelsea. A Johnson brace helped us to a 3-1 home win over Southampton as new loan signing Mathys Tel scored his first league goal in our colours from the penalty spot in stoppage time at the end of the 90. Tel was on target from open play in our 2-4 loss at Wolverhampton Wanderers the following weekend – a game in which Richarlison also scored. The Brazilian netted against Nottingham Forest too in a 1-2 home loss while Solanke gave us the lead before we went down to a heavy 1-5 defeat at Anfield on the day Liverpool won the Premier League title.

PREMIER LEAGUE

2024/25

May

Wilson Odobert's first Premier League goal for us saw us draw 1-1 at West Ham United. We were also beaten 0-2 at home to Crystal Palace and away to Aston Villa. The league campaign ended with a 1-4 loss against Brighton & Hove Albion – a game in which Solanke's ninth-minute penalty gave us the lead.

CUP REVIEWS

In 2024/25, we reached the semi-finals of the Carabao Cup and the fourth round of the Emirates FA Cup.

EMIRATES FA CUP

Tamworth 0-3 Spurs (AET)

Third Round – 12 January, 2025

After being pushed all the way by National League side Tamworth, we were able to settle a tough tie in extra-time. An own goal from Tamworth's Nathan Tshikuna in the 101st minute finally broke the deadlock and we added goals in the second period of extra-time from Dejan Kulusevski and Brennan Johnson.

Spurs: Kinský, Pedro Porro, Drăgușin (Spence 90), Gray, Reguilon, Bissouma, Sarr (Bergvall 68), Maddison (c) (Kulusevski 90), Johnson, Werner (Son 90), Moore (Solanke 68)

Aston Villa 2-1 Spurs

Fourth Round – 9 February, 2025

During a season in which they went on a run to the quarter-finals of the UEFA Champions League, Aston Villa eliminated us from the Emirates FA Cup. A goal in each half from the home side did the damage, with Jacob Ramsey firing Villa into the lead inside the first minute before Morgan Rogers doubled their advantage midway through the second period. Mathys Tel's first Spurs goal proved to be nothing more than a consolation as we exited a second cup competition in four days.

Spurs: Kinský, Pedro Porro, Danso, Gray, Spence, Bentancur (Sarr 72), Bergvall, Kulusevski, Moore (Bissouma 46), Son (c), Tel

CARABAO CUP

Coventry City 1-2 Spurs

Third Round – 18 September, 2024

Two goals in four minutes right at the end of the game gave us a dramatic 2-1 victory over Coventry City on our first-ever visit to the Coventry Building Society Arena.

The Sky Blues took a deserved lead through Brandon Thomas-Asante just after the hour mark, but we produced a late turnaround as Djed Spence opened his Spurs goalscoring account in the 88th minute before Brennan Johnson coolly slotted home the winner two minutes into stoppage time.

Spurs: Forster, Gray, Drăgușin, Davies (c), Udogie (Spence 46), Bentancur, Sarr, Bergvall (Maddison 62), Odobert (Johnson 18), Solanke (Son 62), Werner (Kulusevski 74)

Spurs 2-1 Manchester City

Fourth Round – 30 October, 2024

Timo Werner scored a fantastic goal to give us a fifth-minute lead against Manchester City – a lead which was enhanced further thanks to an equally impressive finish from Pape Matar Sarr. The visitors pulled one back on the stroke of half-time through Matheus Nunes but a spirited second half display saw us through to the quarter-finals.

Spurs: Vicario, Gray, Romero (c) (Davies 52), Drăgușin, van de Ven (Udogie 14), Sarr (Bissouma 46), Bentancur, Kulusevski, Johnson (Moore 68), Solanke, Werner (Richarlison 69)

Spurs 4-3 Manchester United

Quarter-final – 19 December, 2024

Dominic Solanke scored twice as we held off a Manchester United comeback to book our place in the Carabao Cup semi-finals.

Our centre-forward set us on the way with a smart finish after 15 minutes and after Dejan Kulusevski and Solanke had both netted in the opening 10 minutes of the second half, we looked like we were comfortably on our way to the last four. But United came storming back, with substitutes Joshua Zirkzee and Amad Diallo capitalising on goalkeeping errors to score twice in seven minutes to leave the game in the balance. The drama continued as Heung-Min Son scored direct from a corner in the 87th minute before Jonny Evans headed home a corner deep into stoppage time to ensure we had to fight until the end for a famous victory.

Spurs: Forster, Pedro Porro, Drăgușin, Gray, Spence (Reguilon 90+1), Sarr, Bissouma, Maddison (Bergvall 79), Kulusevski, Solanke (Johnson 90), Son (c)

Spurs 1-0 Liverpool

Semi-final – First Leg – 8 January, 2025

Lucas Bergvall scored his first Spurs goal – finishing clinically from Dominic Solanke's brilliant assist on 86 minutes – to give us a 1-0 victory in the first leg of our Carabao Cup semi-final against Liverpool. Debutant goalkeeper Antonín Kinský was in fine form on the night, making a number of excellent saves – including one to deny Darwin Nunez late on to preserve our advantage ahead of the second leg at Anfield.

Spurs: Kinský, Pedro Porro, Drăgușin, Gray, Spence, Bissouma, Bentancur (Johnson 15), Bergvall, Kulusevski, Solanke, Son (c) (Werner 72)

Liverpool 4-0 Spurs

Semi-final – Second Leg – 6 February, 2025

Our Carabao Cup adventure came to an end against a scintillating Liverpool at Anfield. Cody Gakpo levelled the aggregate score in the first half before a Mohamed Salah penalty and goals from Dominik Szoboszlai and Virgil van Dijk completed the Reds' victory and their progression to the final against Newcastle United.

Spurs: Kinský, Gray, Danso, Davies (Moore 84), Spence, Bentancur, Bissouma (Pedro Porro 57), Sarr (Bergvall 57), Kulusevski, Richarlison (Tel 45+1), Son (c)

CARABAO CUP

SPURS WOMEN

SEASON REVIEW 2024/25

The 2024/25 Barclays Women's Super League (WSL) season was a tough one for Spurs Women, but our fighting spirit saw us secure top flight status for the sixth campaign in a row.

Bethany England topped our WSL goalscoring charts with eight strikes while Drew Spence chipped in with three.

Here we look back at how the season unfolded…

SEPTEMBER

Spurs Women made an impressive start to the campaign, thrashing newcomers Crystal Palace 4-0 at Brisbane Road. Hayley Raso scored the opener on her competitive debut for the Club before Jess Naz made it 2-0 shortly after the break. Drew Spence extended our lead and Olga Ahtinen rounded off the scoring with a spectacular long-distance strike with two minutes of the 90 remaining.

A stoppage-time goal from Bethany England saw us return home from Villa Park with a share of the spoils a week later. We'd taken the lead through an Eveliina Summanen penalty after Spence was brought down in the area by Paula Tomas, but Villa drew level on 78 minutes. It looked like the hosts had snatched victory when they netted again 10 minutes later, but a dramatic end to the game saw England head home from Amanda Nildén's cross in the sixth minute of stoppage time to make it 2-2.

OCTOBER

A closely fought contest against Liverpool at Brisbane Road ended in the Reds' favour. The visitors went in front early on before a Taylor Hinds own-goal saw us draw level. Marie Hobinger restored the Reds' lead but Clare Hunt's strike on 83 minutes got us back in the game as we looked to extend our unbeaten league run to three games. It wasn't to be though, as five minutes into stoppage time Hobinger converted from the penalty spot after Ashleigh Neville fouled Sophie Roman Haug in the box, to give Liverpool the win.

Our following two games ended in defeat too as we lost 0-3 at Manchester United and 2-5 at Chelsea, where Nildén and Summanen scored our goals.

NOVEMBER

We put a disappointing October behind us with a 2-1 victory over West Ham United at home. We went behind to a Riko Ueki header in the first half but our women rallied, and Bethany England equalised shortly into the second period. Then, two minutes into stoppage time an own-goal from the Hammers' Camila Saez gave us all three points.

Two tough games followed that victory, as we lost 0-4 at Manchester City and 0-3 to Arsenal at Tottenham Hotspur Stadium in the north London derby.

DECEMBER

A Bethany England brace against Everton at Brisbane Road saw us return to winning ways in the WSL in December. Our captain fired home from close range to give us the lead before Sara Holmgaard equalised for the Toffees shortly before the break. England coolly slotted home the winner from the penalty spot minutes after the restart following a foul on Amanda Nildén.

England's goalscoring streak continued in our final league game of 2024 as we picked up a point in a 1-1 draw at Brighton & Hove Albion.

JANUARY

Our women kicked off the new year with a victory as we beat Leicester City 1-0 at home courtesy of a first-half own-goal from the Foxes' Janina Leitzig. And we made it two wins from two a week later as we played out a five-goal thriller at Crystal Palace.

England scored twice within the first 23 minutes to give Spurs a comfortable lead, but the Eagles fought back early in the second half to level the scores through Katie Stengel and Ashleigh Weerden. Five minutes into added time, Jess Naz was pulled down on the edge of the box and debutant Olivia Holdt stepped up to take the free-kick. The midfielder struck a beautiful curling effort into the top corner to give Spurs their fifth win of the WSL campaign.

FEBRUARY

Manchester United took an early lead on their visit to Tottenham Hotspur Stadium in February and try as they might our women couldn't find the leveller, as our six-game unbeaten run in the WSL came to an end.

We also lost 0-5 to Arsenal at the Emirates Stadium.

MARCH

March was another month to forget as we picked up just one point out of a possible 12.

Bethany England made the scoresheet against Manchester City at Brisbane Road, but goals from Vivianne Miedema and Aoba Fujino saw the visitors run out 1-2 victors.

A 0-1 defeat at home to Brighton was followed by a 0-2 loss on the road at West Ham. But, we did snatch a point from our trip to the King Power Stadium to end our five-match losing streak. Drew Spence finished from close range just after the hour mark to cancel out Josefine Rybrink's own-goal.

APRIL

An end-to-end match with Aston Villa at Brisbane Road ended with the Villans edging us 2-3. Goals from Anna Patten and Ebony Salmon had the visitors two up just 11 minutes after the restart. However, we fought back to get ourselves back on terms as Jess Naz and Ella Morris, with her first goal for the Club, netted. But Villa snatched all three points with a Kirsty Hanson winner in stoppage time.

After Sophie Roman Haug's opener for Liverpool at St Helens Stadium, an own-goal from Rachael Laws and a strike from Clare Hunt saw us lead just after the hour mark. But Liverpool levelled six minutes after the break, when Haug grabbed her second of the game as the clash finished in a 2-2 draw.

MAY

Our final two games of the WSL season saw us lose 0-1 to Chelsea before our campaign concluded with a 1-1 draw at Everton as Drew Spence scored her third goal of the season.

That result meant we were still the only WSL team to never have lost on the final day of the season. But, with five wins, five draws and 12 defeats throughout the campaign we finished a disappointing 11th in the league with 20 points – the same as Leicester City above us but they had a better goal difference.

FACE TO FACE WITH GLORY

BOOK ONLINE AND SAVE 15%

SCAN TO BOOK

WOMEN'S CUP REVIEWS

In 2024/25, we reached the quarter-finals of the Subway Women's League Cup and the fourth round of the Adobe Women's FA Cup.

2024/25 SUBWAY WOMEN'S LEAGUE CUP

Charlton Athletic 1-2 Spurs

Group Stage – 2 October, 2024

Jess Naz netted a late winner to ensure we began our 2024/25 Women's League Cup campaign with a victory. Luana Bühler opened the scoring just eight minutes into the match as she headed home her first goal in our colours but, on the stroke of half-time, Katie Bradley grabbed an equaliser as she converted Ellie Brazil's low cross.

After a relatively quiet second half, it looked destined that the game would be heading to a penalty shootout for an extra point at The Valley. But Naz, who was introduced as a substitute for Matilda Vinberg midway through the second half, had other ideas, firing home the winning goal four minutes from time.

Spurs: Talbert, Neville, Bartrip, Bühler (Hunt 57), Grant, Ahtinen (Dennis 67), Oroz (Summanen 46), Gunning-Williams, Csiki (Spence 68), England (c), Vinberg (Naz 67)

Spurs 1-0 Aston Villa

Group Stage – 23 November, 2024

Eveliina Summanen's Goal of the Season-winning strike (read more about this on page 48!) made it two wins out of two for us in the 2024/25 Women's League Cup.

A moment of magic was needed at Brisbane Road to separate the sides and Summanen certainly delivered that, striking the ball into the top right corner of the Villa net from almost 40 yards out!

Spurs: Heeps, Morris, Bartrip, James-Turner, Nildén, Summanen, Csiki, Naz (Vinberg 81), Thomas, Raso (Neville 89), England (c)

Crystal Palace 0-2 Spurs

Group Stage – 11 December, 2024

A stunning strike from Araya Dennis against her former club sealed a 2-0 win at Crystal Palace and rubber-stamped our place in the next round of the Women's League Cup as we finished top of Group E.

The youngster stepped off the bench and curled home a superb effort on the turn with 19 minutes remaining at the VBS Community Stadium in Sutton, her first goal on only her second appearance for us. That added to Matilda Vinberg's first goal of the season shortly after half-time as we completed the group stage with a 100 per cent record.

Spurs: Heeps, Neville, Bartrip (c), Bühler (Hunt 46), Grant (Bailey 88), Ahtinen, Csiki, Oroz (Wang 46), Vinberg, Gunning-Williams (Dennis 61), Thomas (England 68)

2024/25 ADOBE WOMEN'S FA CUP

Spurs 1-2 West Ham United

Quarter-final, – 22 January, 2025

Martha Thomas headed home her first goal of the campaign to put us ahead in the opening stages of our quarter-final tie against West Ham at Brisbane Road. But two goals in five minutes from Seraina Piubel and Kirsty Smith turned the game in the Hammers' favour on the stroke of half-time.

We pushed for an equaliser in the second half, with Thomas and Vinberg both denied by smart saves from the visitors' goalkeeper Megan Walsh, but we ultimately couldn't find the breakthrough as West Ham progressed to face Chelsea in the semi-final.

Spurs: Heeps, Neville, Hunt, Bartrip, Nildén (Grant 46), Spence, Oroz (Ahtinen 46), Spence, Naz, Raso (Vinberg 80), England (c)

Everton 2-0 Spurs

Fourth Round – 29 January, 2025

Our 2024/25 Adobe Women's FA Cup journey started and ended at Walton Hall Park as second half goals from Kelly Gago and Heather Payne saw us eliminated from the competition at the hands of WSL rivals, Everton.

We were unfortunate to not get at least one goal on the night. In the second half, substitute Rosella Ayane saw her cross strike the outside of the post while a Clare Hunt header was cleared off the Toffees' goal line.

Spurs: Heeps, Grant, Bühler, Hunt, Nildén (Neville 78), Ahtinen, Csiki (Bartrip 77), Raso (Gunning-Williams 59), Thomas (Ayane 59), Vinberg, Naz (Holdt 78)

WINNERS CROSSWORD

Answers on page 60.

ACROSS

3. Brennan Johnson's goal gave us victory over this Premier League team in the final (10/6)
6. Bundesliga team we met in the quarter-finals (9/9)
10. Our first away opponents of the 2024/25 Europa League season (11)
11. The only team to defeat us in a league phase match in 2024/25 (11)

DOWN

1. We beat this Bundesliga side on matchday seven (10)
2. Our semi-final opponents, who play their home matches roughly 200 kilometres north of the Arctic Circle (4/5)
4. Italian side who we drew 2-2 with at Tottenham Hotspur Stadium in November 2024 (4)
5. Our final league phase opponents in 2024/25 (8)
7. We faced this side at Ibrox on matchday six (7)
8. Alkmaar-based side we played in both the league and knockout phase (2)
9. Our first Europa League opponents of the 2024/25 season (7)

WINNERS WORDSEARCH

J	V	G	Q	Z	A	E	L	M	R
O	B	I	S	S	O	U	M	A	L
H	X	O	C	P	V	A	S	R	V
N	S	O	T	A	K	D	A	A	A
S	R	W	E	C	R	A	R	P	N
O	O	F	H	L	X	I	R	O	D
N	M	N	X	H	D	H	O	R	E
B	E	N	T	A	N	C	U	R	V
R	R	J	O	V	T	K	S	O	E
Z	O	P	M	X	H	V	P	C	N

BENTANCUR **VICARIO** **ROMERO**
BISSOUMA **VAN DE VEN** **PORRO**
JOHNSON **SARR**

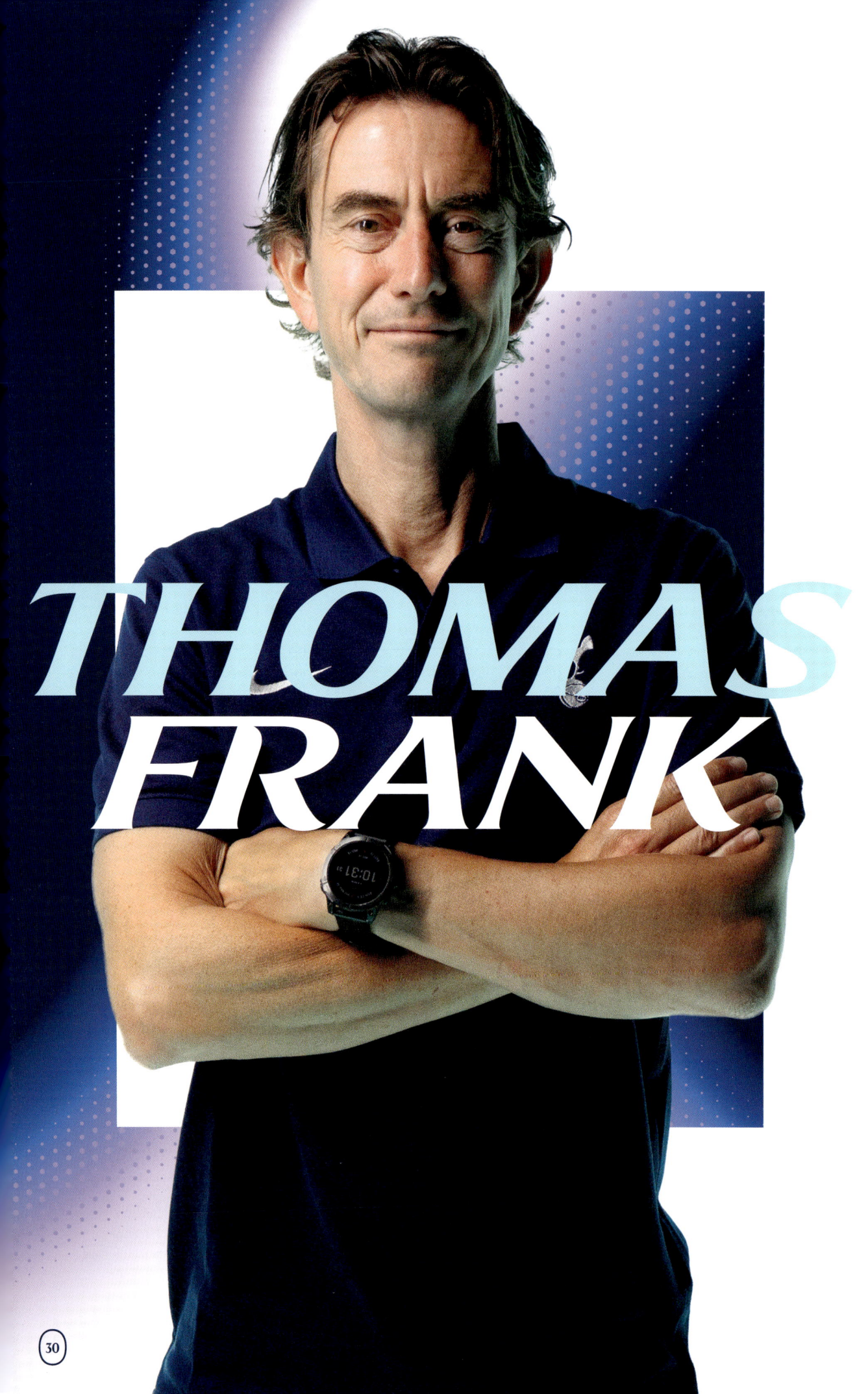

THOMAS FRANK WAS APPOINTED AS OUR MEN'S HEAD COACH IN JUNE 2025

Born in Frederiksværk, Denmark on 9 October, 1973, Thomas had a short playing career in amateur football before beginning his coaching adventure in 1995 with his hometown team, Frederiksværk FK. He initially took charge of the club's U8s and then U12s before future coaching roles with Hvidovre, B93 and Lyngby.

In July 2008, Thomas was appointed manager of the Denmark national U16 and U17 teams and guided the latter to the UEFA European U17 Championship semi-finals in 2011. He was promoted to the role of U19 manager in July 2012 and also presided over U18 and U20 matches on an ad-hoc basis during his five years with the Danish Football Association (DFA). He served as an assistant for Denmark's U16s, U17s and U18s and the women's U17 team on an ad-hoc basis too.

His first senior appointment came with Danish Superliga club Brøndby in June 2013. After Brøndby had finished five points off relegation in the season prior to his arrival, he achieved fourth and third-place finishes in the 2013/14 and 2014/15 seasons respectively, reaching the UEFA Europa League qualifying stages as a result.

Frank was appointed as an assistant head coach at then-Championship side Brentford in December 2016, where he worked under Dean Smith. When Smith departed for Aston Villa in October 2018, Thomas became the Bees' new head coach. In his first full season, the Dane guided Brentford to the Championship Play-Off Final, where they were beaten 2-1 by local rivals, Fulham. A year later, the Bees returned to the showpiece final, beating Swansea City 2-0 to gain their first-ever promotion to the Premier League and just the club's sixth top-flight season since they were formed back in 1889.

Under Frank, the Bees made themselves immediately at home in the Premier League – finishing 13th in their debut campaign in the division in 2021/22 and following that up with a ninth-placed finish in 2022/23. In October 2022, Frank achieved the feat of having won more of his first 200 matches than any Brentford head coach or manager to also reach 200 games, during a season in which the Bees ended up 16th in the Premier League table. And in his final campaign at the Gtech Community Stadium in 2024/25, Brentford once again finished in the division's top 10.

Thomas was accompanied in his move across London in the summer of 2025 by a number of his former colleagues. Justin Cochrane (First Team Assistant Coach), Chris Haslam (Head of Performance & First Team Assistant Coach) and Joe Newton (First Team Coach Analyst) all arrived from Brentford while Andreas Georgson (First Team Assistant Coach) joined from Manchester United, having previously worked under Frank at Brentford between 2019 and 2020.

SPURS MEN 2025/26

POSITION GK | **1** | **LEGACY Nº** 876

GUGLIELMO VICARIO

BORN: 7 OCTOBER, 1996
UDINE, ITALY

PREVIOUS CLUBS: UDINESE, FONTANAFREDDA (LOAN), VENEZIA, CAGLIARI, PERUGIA (LOAN), EMPOLI

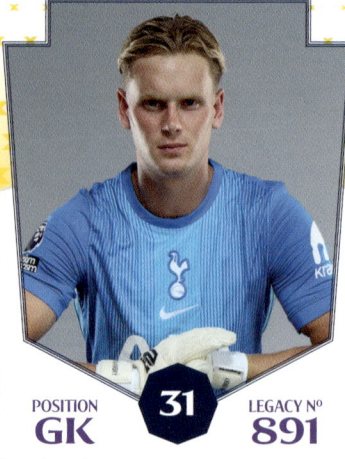

POSITION GK | **31** | **LEGACY Nº** 891

ANTONÍN KINSKÝ

BORN: 13 MARCH, 2003
PRAGUE, CZECH REPUBLIC

PREVIOUS CLUBS: DUKLA PRAGUE, SLAVIA PRAGUE, VYŠKOV (LOAN), PARDUBICE (LOAN)

POSITION GK | **40** | **LEGACY Nº** 890

BRANDON AUSTIN

BORN: 8 JANUARY, 1999
HEMEL HEMPSTEAD, ENGLAND

PREVIOUS CLUBS: VIBORG FF (LOAN), ORLANDO CITY (LOAN)

POSITION DF | **3** | **LEGACY Nº** 882

RADU DRĂGUȘIN

BORN: 3 FEBRUARY, 2002
BUCHAREST, ROMANIA

PREVIOUS CLUBS: JUVENTUS, SAMPDORIA (LOAN), SALERNITANA (LOAN), GENOA

POSITION DF **4** **LEGACY N°** 894

KEVIN DANSO

BORN: 19 SEPTEMBER 1998
VOITSBERG, AUSTRIA

PREVIOUS CLUBS:
FC AUGSBURG, SOUTHAMPTON (LOAN), FORTUNA DÜSSELDORF (LOAN), LENS

AUTOGRAPH

POSITION DF **25** **LEGACY N°** –

KŌTA TAKAI

BORN: 4 SEPTEMBER, 2004
TSURUMI-KU, JAPAN

PREVIOUS CLUB:
KAWASAKI FRONTALE

AUTOGRAPH

POSITION DF **37** **LEGACY N°** 875

MICKY VAN DE VEN

BORN: 19 APRIL, 2001
WORMER, NETHERLANDS

PREVIOUS CLUBS:
VOLENDAM, VFL WOLFSBURG

AUTOGRAPH

POSITION DF   **17** **LEGACY N°** 853

CRISTIAN ROMERO

BORN: 27 APRIL, 1998
CÓRDOBA, ARGENTINA

PREVIOUS CLUBS:
BELGRANO, GENOA, JUVENTUS, ATALANTA

AUTOGRAPH

POSITION DF **23** **LEGACY Nº** 870

PEDRO PORRO

BORN: 13 SEPTEMBER, 1999
DON BENITO, SPAIN

PREVIOUS CLUBS:
PERALADA-GIRONA B, GIRONA, MANCHESTER CITY, VALLADOLID (LOAN), SPORTING CP

POSITION DF **13** **LEGACY Nº** 874

DESTINY UDOGIE

BORN: 28 NOVEMBER, 2002
VERONA, ITALY

PREVIOUS CLUBS:
HELLAS VERONA, UDINESE (LOAN)

POSITION DF **24** **LEGACY Nº** 866

DJED SPENCE

BORN: 9 AUGUST, 2000
LONDON, ENGLAND

PREVIOUS CLUBS:
MIDDLESBROUGH, NOTTINGHAM FOREST (LOAN), RENNES (LOAN), LEEDS UNITED (LOAN), GENOA (LOAN)

POSITION DF **33** **LEGACY Nº** 796

BEN DAVIES

BORN: 24 APRIL, 1993
NEATH, WALES

PREVIOUS CLUB:
SWANSEA CITY

POSITION MF **8** **LEGACY Nº** 864

YVES BISSOUMA

BORN: 30 AUGUST, 1996
ISSIA, IVORY COAST

PREVIOUS CLUBS:
REAL BAMAKO, LILLE,
BRIGHTON & HOVE ALBION

AUTOGRAPH

POSITION MF **6** **LEGACY Nº** 897

JOÃO PALHINHA

BORN: 9 JULY, 1995
LISBON, PORTUGAL

PREVIOUS CLUBS: SPORTING CP B, MOREIRENSE (LOAN), SPORTING CP, BELENENSES (LOAN), SC BRAGA (LOAN), FULHAM, BAYERN MUNICH*

AUTOGRAPH

*ON LOAN FROM BAYERN MUNICH FOR THE 2025/26 SEASON

POSITION MF **29** **LEGACY Nº** 868

PAPE MATAR SARR

BORN: 14 SEPTEMBER, 2002
THIAROYE, SENEGAL

PREVIOUS CLUB:
METZ

AUTOGRAPH

POSITION 14 **LEGACY Nº**
MF 886

ARCHIE GRAY

BORN: 12 MARCH, 2006
DURHAM, ENGLAND

PREVIOUS CLUB:
LEEDS UNITED

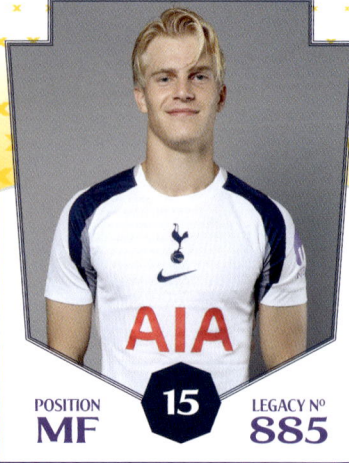

POSITION 15 **LEGACY Nº**
MF 885

LUCAS BERGVALL

BORN: 2 FEBRUARY, 2006
STOCKHOLM, SWEDEN

PREVIOUS CLUBS:
IF BROMMAPOJKARNA, DJURGÅRDEN

POSITION 30 **LEGACY Nº**
MF 861

RODRIGO BENTANCUR

BORN: 25 JUNE, 1997
NUEVA HELVECIA, URUGUAY

PREVIOUS CLUBS:
BOCA JUNIORS, JUVENTUS

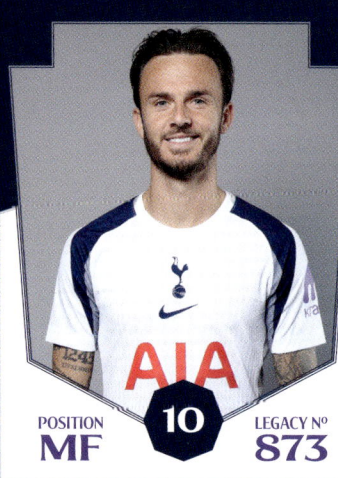

POSITION 10 **LEGACY Nº**
MF 873

JAMES MADDISON

BORN: 23 NOVEMBER, 1996
COVENTRY, ENGLAND

PREVIOUS CLUBS:
COVENTRY CITY, NORWICH CITY, ABERDEEN (LOAN), LEICESTER CITY

POSITION	7	LEGACY Nº
FW		–

XAVI SIMONS

BORN: 21 APRIL, 2003
AMSTERDAM, NETHERLANDS

PREVIOUS CLUBS:
PARIS SAINT-GERMAIN, PSV EINDHOVEN, RB LEIPZIG

AUTOGRAPH

POSITION	21	LEGACY Nº
FW		860

DEJAN KULUSEVSKI

BORN: 25 APRIL, 2000
STOCKHOLM, SWEDEN

PREVIOUS CLUBS:
ATALANTA, PARMA (LOAN), JUVENTUS

AUTOGRAPH

POSITION	11	LEGACY Nº
FW		895

MATHYS TEL

BORN: 27 APRIL, 2005
SARCELLES, FRANCE

PREVIOUS CLUBS:
RENNES, BAYERN MUNICH

AUTOGRAPH

POSITION FW | **28** | **LEGACY Nº** 887

WILSON ODOBERT

BORN: 28 NOVEMBER, 2004
MEAUX, FRANCE

PREVIOUS CLUBS:
TROYES, BURNLEY

AUTOGRAPH

POSITION FW | **39** | **LEGACY Nº** –

RANDAL KOLO MUANI

BORN: 5 DECEMBER 1998
BONDY, FRANCE

PREVIOUS CLUBS:
NANTES B, NANTES, BOULOGNE (LOAN), EINTRACHT FRANKFURT, PARIS SAINT-GERMAIN*

AUTOGRAPH

*ON LOAN FROM PSG FOR THE 2025/26 SEASON

POSITION FW | **22** | **LEGACY Nº** 878

BRENNAN JOHNSON

BORN: 23 MAY, 2001
NOTTINGHAM, ENGLAND

PREVIOUS CLUBS:
NOTTINGHAM FOREST, LINCOLN CITY (LOAN)

AUTOGRAPH

POSITION FW | **44** | **LEGACY Nº** 849

DANE SCARLETT

BORN: 24 MARCH, 2004
HILLINGDON, ENGLAND

PREVIOUS CLUBS:
PORTSMOUTH (LOAN), IPSWICH TOWN (LOAN), OXFORD UNITED (LOAN)

AUTOGRAPH

POSITION FW | **9** | **LEGACY Nº** 865

RICHARLISON

BORN: 10 MAY, 1997
NOVA VENÉCIA, BRAZIL

PREVIOUS CLUBS:
AMÉRICA MINEIRO, FLUMINENSE, WATFORD, EVERTON

AUTOGRAPH

POSITION FW | **19** | **LEGACY Nº** 884

DOMINIC
SOLANKE

BORN: 14 SEPTEMBER, 1997
READING, ENGLAND

PREVIOUS CLUBS:
CHELSEA, VITESSE (LOAN), LIVERPOOL, AFC BOURNEMOUTH

AUTOGRAPH

POSITION FW | **20** | **LEGACY Nº** 896

MOHAMMED
KUDUS

BORN: 2 AUGUST, 2000
NIMA, GHANA

PREVIOUS CLUBS:
NORDSJÆLLAND, AJAX, WEST HAM UNITED

AUTOGRAPH

MARTIN HO

Martin Ho was appointed as our Women's Head Coach in July 2025, signing a contract that runs until 2028.

Born in Liverpool on 6 June, 1990, to a Chinese father and an English mother, Ho was part of Everton's academy for a period as a young player. But for his senior career, his focus shifted to coaching and between 2015 and 2018, Martin worked as Assistant Manager to Andy Spence at Everton Women. He moved across the city in August 2018 to join Liverpool as their Technical Director. In that role, he would oversee the youth set-up at the club and help create a programme to develop and pave out a pathway to senior football for the academy players, with some going on to become regulars in the WSL to this day.

Martin was offered a fresh challenge with Manchester United in January 2020, joining as an assistant coach to former Women's Head Coach Casey Stoney and, in the first two seasons, he helped them to consecutive fourth place finishes in the WSL and the semi-finals of the Women's League Cup during the 2019/20 term.

Following Marc Skinner's arrival in July 2021, he continued to be an integral part of the backroom staff at United, once again obtaining a third consecutive fourth place finish in England's top flight and a place in the final four of the Women's League Cup. In his final season with the Red Devils in 2022/23, United recorded their best-ever finish in the WSL, finishing second, also securing qualification for the UEFA Women's Champions League and reaching the final of the Women's FA Cup – where they lost 1-0 to Chelsea at Wembley.

After leaving United in the summer of 2023, Martin took his first Head Coach role with Norwegian side SK Brann for the remainder of the 2023 Toppserien campaign. He made an immediate impact upon joining the club as, after they endured a difficult start to the season with five defeats in 16 games, he rediscovered their league form with seven wins in his first nine games to help them finish fourth in the table.

He also created history for Brann in the UEFA Women's Champions League during that term, leading them to victory in all four of their qualifying matches to secure a place in the group stage, becoming the first Norwegian side to have reached that stage of the competition. They eventually exited the competition at the quarter-final stage, losing 5-2 to reigning champions, FC Barcelona.

Brann were Toppserien runners-up in Martin's first full season with the club in 2024. The campaign also saw them reach the semi-finals of the Norwegian Women's Cup. The 2025 season kicked off in March with a 3-0 win over Rosenborg which came at the start of an impressive 11-game unbeaten run, in which they defeated champions Valerenga. They also secured their spot in the semi-final of the Women's Cup once again. As Martin departed Norway for Spurs, Brann found themselves in second place, just one point behind the league leaders.

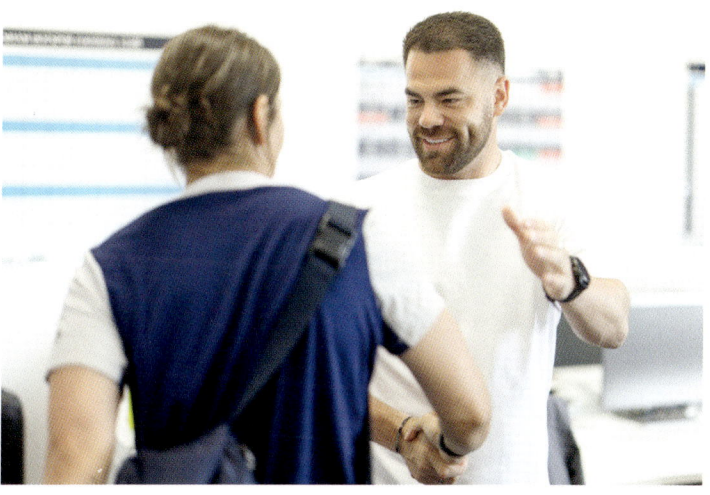

SPURS WOMEN 2025/26

LIZE KOP
24/25 APP: 12 — GK — **24/25 GLS:** 00
BORN: 17 MARCH, 1998
WORMER, NETHERLANDS
PREVIOUS CLUBS: AJAX, LEICESTER CITY

ELEANOR HEEPS
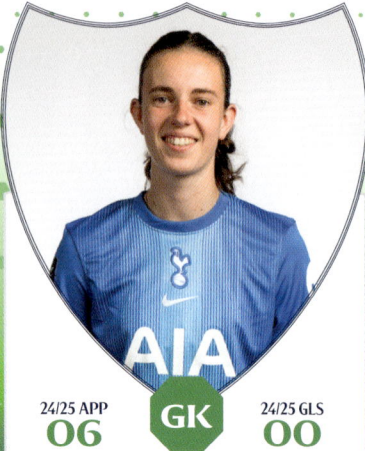
24/25 APP: 06 — GK — **24/25 GLS:** 00
BORN: 4 AUGUST, 2003
CREWE, ENGLAND
PREVIOUS CLUBS: LIVERPOOL, BLACKBURN ROVERS (LOAN), COVENTRY UNITED (LOAN), SHEFFIELD UNITED (LOAN)

ELLA MORRIS

24/25 APP: 13 — DF — **24/25 GLS:** 01
BORN: 23 SEPTEMBER, 2002
SOUTHAMPTON, ENGLAND
PREVIOUS CLUBS: SOUTHAMPTON

AMY JAMES-TURNER

24/25 APP: 02 — DF — **24/25 GLS:** 00
BORN: 4 JULY, 1991
SHEFFIELD, ENGLAND
PREVIOUS CLUBS: HOFSTRA PRIDE, DONCASTER ROVERS BELLES, LEEDS UNITED, SHEFFIELD, LINCOLN LADIES/NOTTS COUNTY, LIVERPOOL, MANCHESTER UNITED, ORLANDO PRIDE

24/25 APP **27** DF 24/25 GLS **00**

MOLLY BARTRIP

BORN: 1 JUNE, 1996
ROMFORD, ENGLAND

PREVIOUS CLUB:
READING

24/25 APP **19** DF 24/25 GLS **01**

AMANDA NILDÉN

BORN: 7 AUGUST, 1998
STOCKHOLM, SWEDEN

PREVIOUS CLUBS:
IF BROMMAPOJKARNA, AIK, BRIGHTON & HOVE ALBION, ESKILSTUNA UNITED, JUVENTUS

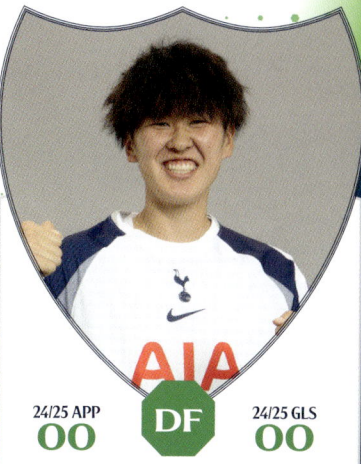

24/25 APP **00** DF 24/25 GLS **00**

TŌKO KOGA

BORN: 6 JANUARY, 2006
OSAKA, JAPAN

PREVIOUS CLUBS:
JFA ACADEMY FUKUSHIMA, FEYENOORD

24/25 APP **14** DF 24/25 GLS **00**

CHARLOTTE GRANT

BORN: 20 SEPTEMBER, 2001
ADELAIDE, AUSTRALIA

PREVIOUS CLUBS:
ADELAIDE UNITED, ROSENGÅRD, VITTSJÖ

24/25 APP **26** DF 24/25 GLS **00**

ASHLEIGH NEVILLE

BORN: 29 APRIL, 1993
WEST BROMWICH, ENGLAND

PREVIOUS CLUBS:
SPORTING CLUB ALBION, COVENTRY UNITED

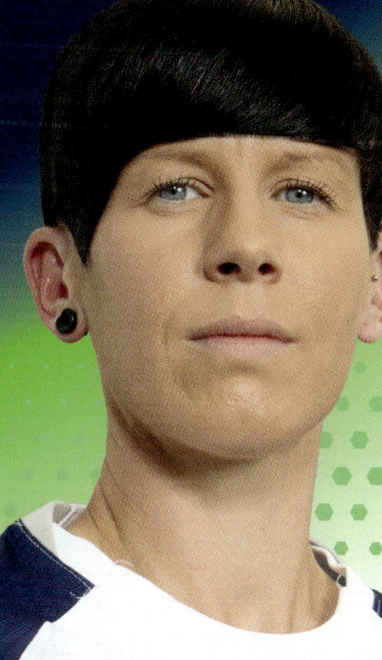

24/25 APP **06** | DF | 24/25 GLS **00**

JOSEFINE RYBRINK

BORN: 19 JANUARY, 1998
ONSALA, SWEDEN

PREVIOUS CLUBS:
KUNGSBACKA, KRISTIANSTADS, BK HÄCKEN

24/25 APP **09** | DF | 24/25 GLS **01**

LUANA BÜHLER

BORN: 28 APRIL, 1996
LUCERNE, SWITZERLAND

PREVIOUS CLUBS:
FC ZÜRICH, 1899 HOFFENHEIM

24/25 APP **21** | DF | 24/25 GLS **02**

CLARE HUNT

BORN: 12 MARCH, 1999
GRENFELL, AUSTRALIA

PREVIOUS CLUBS:
CANBERRA UNITED, WESTERN SYDNEY WANDERERS, PARIS SAINT-GERMAIN

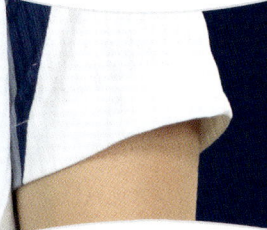

24/25 APP **19** | MF | 24/25 GLS **00**

MAITE OROZ

BORN: 25 MARCH, 1998
HUARTE, SPAIN

PREVIOUS CLUBS:
OSASUNA, ATHLETIC CLUB B, ATHLETIC CLUB, REAL MADRID

24/25 APP **13** MF 24/25 GLS **00**

ANNA
CSIKI

BORN: 14 NOVEMBER, 1999
BUDAPEST, HUNGARY

PREVIOUS CLUBS:
FERENCVÁROS, BK HÄCKEN

AUTOGRAPH

24/25 APP **16** MF 24/25 GLS **01**

OLGA
AHTINEN

BORN: 15 AUGUST, 1997
KOKKOLA, FINLAND

PREVIOUS CLUBS:
GBK, KOKKOLA FUTIS 10, PALLOKISSAT, PK-35 VANTAA, BRØNDBY IF, IF LIMHAMN BUNKEFLO, LINKÖPINGS FC

AUTOGRAPH

24/25 APP **19** MF 24/25 GLS **03**

EVELIINA
SUMMANEN

BORN: 29 MAY, 1998
LAPPEENRANTA, FINLAND

PREVIOUS CLUBS:
HJK, KIF ÖREBRO, KRISTIANSTADS

AUTOGRAPH

24/25 APP **21** 24/25 GLS **03**

DREW
SPENCE

BORN: 23 OCTOBER, 1992
LONDON, ENGLAND

PREVIOUS CLUB:
CHELSEA

AUTOGRAPH

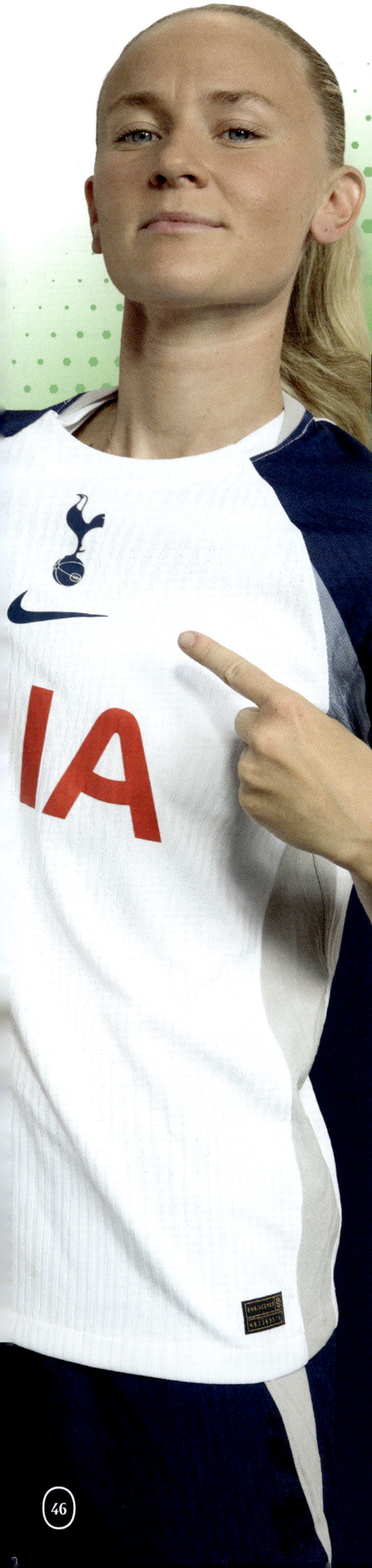

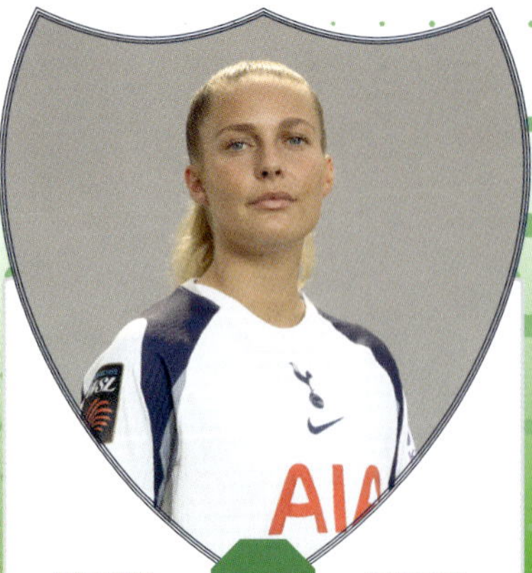

24/25 APP 12 | MF | 24/25 GLS 01

OLIVIA
HOLDT

BORN: 7 JUNE, 2001
IKAST, DENMARK

PREVIOUS CLUBS:
VSK AARHUS, FORTUNA HJØRRING, FC ROSENGÅRD

AUTOGRAPH

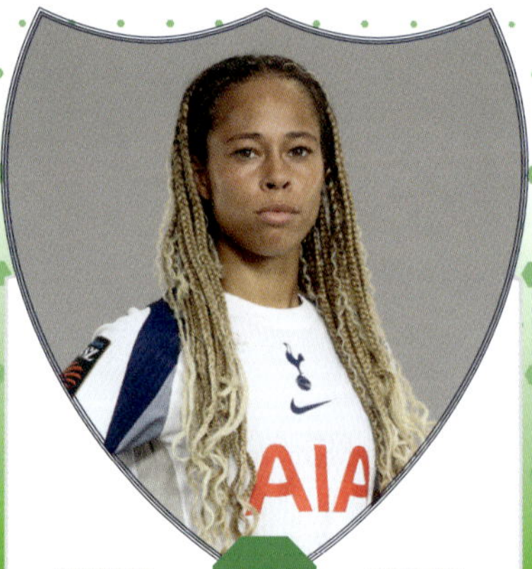

24/25 APP 16 | FW | 24/25 GLS 00

LENNA
GUNNING-WILLIAMS

BORN: 5 FEBRUARY, 2005
LONDON, ENGLAND

PREVIOUS CLUB:
IPSWICH TOWN (LOAN)

AUTOGRAPH

24/25 APP 23 | FW | 24/25 GLS 01

MATILDA
VINBERG

BORN: 16 MARCH, 2003
STOCKHOLM, SWEDEN

PREVIOUS CLUBS:
ENSKEDE IK, HAMMARBY IF

AUTOGRAPH

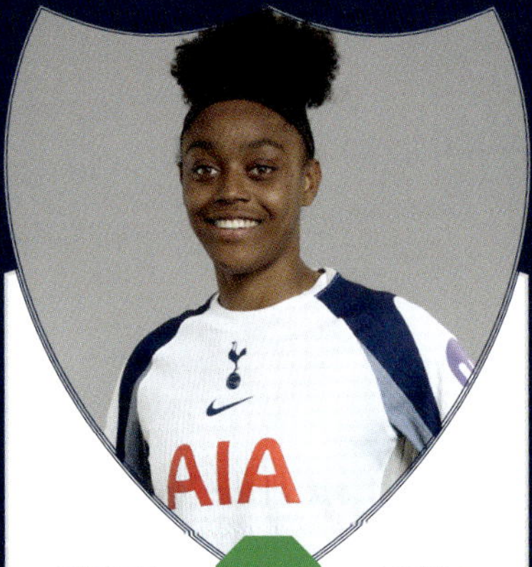

24/25 APP 02 | FW | 24/25 GLS 01

ARAYA
DENNIS

BORN: 11 JANUARY, 2006
LONDON, ENGLAND

PREVIOUS CLUBS:
ARSENAL, WATFORD (LOAN), CRYSTAL PALACE (LOAN), SOUTHAMPTON (LOAN)

AUTOGRAPH

24/25 APP: 26 | FW | 24/25 GLS: 01

MARTHA THOMAS

BORN: 31 MAY, 1996
MALMESBURY, ENGLAND

PREVIOUS CLUBS: CHARLOTTE 49ERS, LE HAVRE, WEST HAM UNITED, MANCHESTER UNITED

AUTOGRAPH

24/25 APP: 26 | FW | 24/25 GLS: 03

JESSICA NAZ

BORN: 23 SEPTEMBER, 2000
LONDON, ENGLAND

PREVIOUS CLUB: ARSENAL

AUTOGRAPH

24/25 APP: 00 | FW | 24/25 GLS: 00

KIT GRAHAM

BORN: 11 NOVEMBER, 1995
CHATHAM, ENGLAND

PREVIOUS CLUB: CHARLTON ATHLETIC

AUTOGRAPH

24/25 APP: 23 |  FW | 24/25 GLS: 08

BETHANY ENGLAND

BORN: 3 JUNE, 1994
BARNSLEY, ENGLAND

PREVIOUS CLUBS: DONCASTER ROVERS BELLES, SHEFFIELD WEDNESDAY (LOAN), CHELSEA, LIVERPOOL (LOAN)

AUTOGRAPH

PLAYER OF THE SEASON AWARDS 2024/25

In his maiden season as a Spurs player, Lucas Bergvall completed a clean sweep of the Club's Men's Player of the Season awards in 2024/25.

The Swedish midfielder was named Player of the Season by our Official Supporters' Clubs (OSC) as well as well as both One Hotspur Members and One Hotspur Juniors. Aged just 19 when he picked up his awards, Bergvall became the first Spurs teenager since Glenn Hoddle (also 19 years old) to receive such an accolade.

Having joined us from Swedish side Djurgarden in the summer of 2024, Lucas made his debut at Leicester City in our opening game of the 2024/25 season. He went on to feature in 45 matches during the campaign and opened his goalscoring account with the match-winner in a 1-0 victory over Liverpool in the Carabao Cup semi-final first leg at Tottenham Hotspur Stadium in January 2025. He signed a new contract with us in April 2025 which will run through until 2031.

Bethany England, Ella Morris and Eveliina Summanen were all recognised with awards on the back of their performances for Spurs Women in 2024/25.

Our skipper Bethany was awarded the Adult Supporters' Player of the Season while Ella – after an impressive maiden campaign in N17 – was named the Junior Supporters' Player of the Season. Eveliina picked up the fan-voted Goal of the Season award for her stunning strike against Aston Villa in the Women's League Cup in November 2024.

ONE CLUB

ONE HOTSPUR MEMBERSHIP 2025/26

PRIORITY TICKET ACCESS FOR PREMIER LEAGUE & CHAMPIONS LEAGUE

15% SPURS SHOP DISCOUNT ON SELECTED MEMBER DAYS

ACCESS TO ONE HOTSPUR MOMENTS, EVENTS AND EXPERIENCES

RETAIL GIFT VOUCHER

GIFT VOUCHERS FOR VISITOR ATTRACTIONS

SEASON TICKET WAITING LIST POSITION

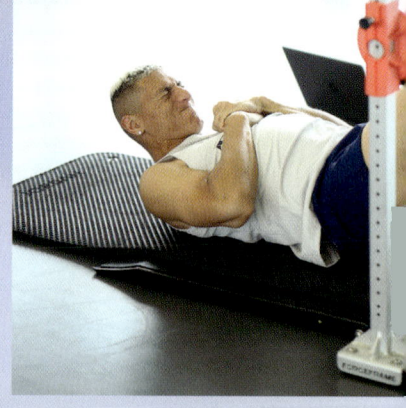

BACK IN

The team at Hotspur Way preparing for the start of the 2025/26 season

BUSINESS!

PRE-SEASON ROUND-UP
SUMMER 2025

Reading 0-2 Spurs

Select Car Leasing Stadium, 19 July, 2025

A bumper crowd was present at the Select Car Leasing Stadium as Spurs supporters were given the first opportunity to see their UEFA Europa League-winning team in action post-Bilbao. In Thomas Frank's first game as Head Coach, second half goals from Will Lankshear and Luka Vušković – in his first outing in a Spurs shirt – gave us victory in Berkshire.

Spurs 2-2 Wycombe Wanderers

Hotspur Way, 26 July, 2025

We hosted League One side Wycombe Wanderers in a behind closed doors friendly at Hotspur Way as preparations for the new season continued. Pape Matar Sarr gave us the lead after 14 minutes before Junior Quitirna equalised on 32 minutes. After the break Quitirna scored again for Wycombe and Sarr netted once more for Spurs as the match ended all square.

Luton Town 0-0 Spurs

Kenilworth Road, 26 July, 2025

On the same day we faced Wycombe at Hotspur Way, another first team squad travelled to Kenilworth Road to take on former Premier League side, Luton Town. The hosts had more chances overall, with Nahki Wells denied by a superb save from Antonin Kinsky at the start of the second half while at the other end, Mohammed Kudus had a shot blocked on the line and Lankshear dragged a late opportunity wide.

Arsenal 0-1 Spurs

Kai Tak Sports Park, Kowloon, Hong Kong, 31 July, 2025

An historic, first-ever north London derby to be played outside of the United Kingdom was settled by an incredible long-range goal from Sarr just before the half-time interval. The Senegal international midfielder spotted Arsenal goalkeeper David Raya off his goalline and duly floated a shot over his head from all of 45 yards, which nestled in the back of the net.

It was so nearly 2-0 in the 66th minute when Mathys Tel, one of three substitutes to come on a few minutes earlier, sent over a wonderful cross to the back post, only for Micky van de Ven to head just wide. A crowd of 49,975 watched the all-Premier League clash inside the Kai Tak Sports Park.

Spurs 1-1 Newcastle

Seoul World Cup Stadium, South Korea, 3 August, 2025

An emotional day at the Seoul World Cup Stadium saw Heung-Min Son make his final appearance for us after an incredible decade-long Spurs career. And it seemed fitting that his swansong should come at the Seoul World Cup Stadium – a venue where he has captained the South Korea national team on many occasions.

Following his prior announcement that he would be leaving the Club, Son was selected to start by Thomas Frank and led our players onto the pitch prior to kick-off as captain. Sonny was substituted on the 64th minute to rapturous applause from the 64,773 fans as well as the players and staff of both teams.

In terms of the match itself, Brennan Johnson's early goal was cancelled out by Harvey Barnes. Sadly, James Maddison sustained an injury in the game that subsequently saw him ruled out for the majority of the 2025/26 campaign.

Bayern Munich 4-0 Spurs

Allianz Arena, Munich, Germany, 7 August, 2025

Our final pre-season friendly ended in defeat in Germany as Bayern Munich ran out 4-0 winners with our former striker Harry Kane among the goalscorers.

Kane opened the scoring early on before second-half goals from Kingsley Coman, Lennart Karl and Jonah Kusi-Asare saw Bayern claim the Telekom Cup.

There were a number of players in action against their former clubs, with João Palhinha making his first appearance in our colours against his parent club following his recent loan move, while Mathys Tel also returned to Munich after signing permanently for us in the summer. And, of course, our all-time top goalscorer Kane was in Bayern's starting XI.

Spurs supporter Kidwild – born Keaton Edmund – rose to fame playing Freddie in hit children's TV football show Jamie Johnson - coincidentally, created and written by fellow Spurs fan, Dan Freedman. He featured in 42 episodes between 2019-2022, where he regularly starred alongside current Spurs Women forward, Lenna-Gunning Williams.

Kidwild's rapping first caught the eye via TikTok in 2022 and he released Distro Kid, a five-track EP with headline tracks Redemption (feat. Nemzzz) and Indecisive - Is It A Crime, in 2025. And it was Redemption which provided the soundtrack for a motivational video Spurs released across our social channels prior to the 2025 UEFA Europa League Final.

At the time of writing, Kidwild had two million monthly streams on Spotify and approaching half a million followers on social media. While he's busier than ever, Keaton says he will "always watch every Spurs match", be that on TV or in person at Tottenham Hotspur Stadium, having first attended a game back in the mid-2010s.

Ahead of the start of the 2025/26 season, we spoke to Kidwild about his music career, love for Spurs and Europa League glory…

Hi Keaton. First of all, can you tell us how you became a Spurs supporter?
I had a friend at school whose dad had season tickets at Spurs for three people. Only him and his son used to go regularly, so I'd get the opportunity to go with them.

What was your first Spurs match?
When I'm asked, I always struggle to remember what my first Spurs game was. I've got photos from the game, which I need to find to remember for sure. I'm pretty sure it was against Leicester and I know we won. I reckon we're talking 2014 or 2015. I remember getting to a league match at Wembley when we were in between our move from White Hart Lane to our current stadium too. Again, I can't remember who we were playing. I always get a programme when I go to a game, so I need to dig those out to jog my memory!

What have been your highlights supporting Spurs over the years?

There was our final season at White Hart Lane in 2016/17, when we were unbeaten there and finished second in the Premier League. There was the great game against Ajax in 2019 to get us to the Champions League Final. But definitely, definitely, my biggest highlight was winning the Europa League last season. I had a track of mine called Redemption on the promo video that Spurs released for the final on their socials, so that was a nice personal connection for me too. Spurs were on the lookout for a motivational track and a lot of people tell me that song in particular motivates them, so it was a perfect match. I changed some of the lyrics for the Spurs video and I loved how it all came together.

I watched all the matches en route to the final on TV and I got to the first leg of the semi-final against Bodø/Glimt. What an atmosphere it was that night... the best atmosphere I think I've experienced at Tottenham Hotspur Stadium. I was at home watching the final and there was a period when the wi-fi cut out. Suddenly, the signal was back and I could see people celebrating and I had to watch it back to see the goal. But it didn't spoil it for me too much... what a night it was!

Who have been your favourite Spurs players over the years?

Shall we go for a top three?! I'm saying, Harry Kane, Heung-Min Son and James Maddison in that order. We know all about what Kane and Son have achieved for this Club and I've always been a big fan of James Maddison since he joined us. How incredible was it to see Sonny get his hands on that Europa League trophy?! And Maddison too. And in the same season Kane won his first big trophy with Bayern Munich.

How often do you get to matches these days?

I went to six matches in 2024/25. If I'm not there, I'm always watching us on the laptop. The Bodø/Glimt match was the highlight for me last season as I say in terms of matches I was at!

Can you tell us a bit about your music career to date, how you made the breakthrough and some of your highlights along the way?

I was away from home, spending three months in Wales (filming for the Jamie Johnson television series). I was bored when I was done on set, so I ordered a recording mic on Amazon. It was probably the worst mic you could ever order, but it didn't matter. I plugged it in to my laptop and started rapping over YouTube beats.

I probably made about 80 songs in that three-month period, but there was only one song I was happy with, which I sent to all of my friends. I got some good feedback so I started posting it. I dropped the music video on TikTok and it went viral in different countries. I could never have expected that to have happened having just purchased a mic off the internet.

That first song remains so important to me. Towards the end of 2024, that was when I started getting loads of listeners, doing more live shows etc. Performing live is incredible. I can remember myself and another artist, Nemzzz, performing Redemption at PRYZM Kingston, everyone was singing the words back to us, word for word. It was amazing.

How much of a dream is it to hear your music played at Tottenham Hotspur Stadium one day?

I've been going to Spurs matches for over 10 years, so that would be the ultimate for me!

How do you describe your music?

I'd describe my music as a feeling. All music, you get a feeling for, but I think mine offers authenticity. My lyrics come from the things I've been through and where I'm from. People can relate to the music and the words I'm speaking. If I had to describe my music in three words, I'd say hope, realness and uplifting.

SUPER SPURS QUIZ

Test your knowledge of your favourite club with these 20 questions...

Answers on page 60.

1. Who scored twice in our 3-1 win over AZ in our UEFA Europa League round of 16, second leg tie in March 2025?

2. What nationality are Charli Grant, Hayley Raso and Clare Hunt?

3. Which Premier League club did our Men's side beat four times in all competitions during the 2024/25 season?

4. By what scoreline did we beat then-reigning champions Manchester City at the Etihad Stadium in a Premier League match in November 2024?

5. Our run to the Carabao Cup semi-finals in 2024/25 began with victory over which Championship side in the third round?

6. In which Spanish city did we play the 2025 UEFA Europa League Final?

7. What number shirt did Bethany England wear during the 2024/25 season?

8. At which Birmingham-based stadium did Spurs Women play their first WSL away match in 2024/25?

9. Which two WSL teams did Spurs Women play at Tottenham Hotspur Stadium during 2024/25?

10. What prestigious match did Spurs Women compete in for the first time in May 2024?

11. Which stadium was our temporary home between 2017 and 2019?

12. With 18 goals in all competitions, who was our Men's top scorer in 2024/25?

13. Which position does Lize Kop play?

14. In what year were Spurs Women promoted to the WSL?

15. Who do Brennan Johnson and Ben Davies play international football for?

16. As of the start of the 2025/26 season, how many times had our Men's team won the FA Cup?

17. Which French club provided our opponents for the 2025 UEFA Super Cup?

18. Prior to 2025, what year did we last win the UEFA Europa League, then known as the UEFA Cup?

19. Based on the short road at its entrance, by what name is our Training Centre often referred to?

20. In English, what does the club's Latin motto Audere est Facere roughly translate as?

QUIZ ANSWERS

PAGE 28
CROSSWORD

PAGE 29
WORDSEARCH

J	V	G	Q	Z	A	E	L	M	R
O	B	I	S	S	O	U	M	A	L
H	X	O	C	P	V	A	S	R	V
N	S	O	T	A	K	D	A	A	A
S	R	W	E	C	R	A	R	P	N
O	O	F	H	L	X	I	R	O	D
N	M	N	X	H	D	H	O	R	E
B	E	N	T	A	N	C	U	R	V
R	R	J	O	V	T	K	S	O	E
Z	O	P	M	X	H	V	P	C	N

PAGE 58-59
SUPER SPURS QUIZ

1. Wilson Odobert
2. Australian
3. Manchester United
4. 4-0
5. Coventry City
6. Bilbao
7. Nine
8. Villa Park
9. Arsenal and Manchester United
10. Women's FA Cup Final
11. Wembley Stadium
12. Brennan Johnson
13. Goalkeeper
14. 2019
15. Wales
16. Eight
17. Paris Saint-Germain
18. 1984
19. Hotspur Way
20. To Dare Is To Do